The Brilliant Barber Bus

Richard O'Neill & Michelle Russell
Jade Van Der Zalm

Collins

Contents

THE BUS 2

MEET THE BARBER BUS TEAM! 4

Chapter 1: Summer adventures 7

Chapter 2: Toady 17

Chapter 3: To Cumbersdale! 27

Chapter 4: Trapped! 37

Chapter 5: Rescue 47

Chapter 6: Guests of honour 55

THE BUS TRIP 64

ALL KINDS OF HAIR 66

TRAVELLERS' TALES 68

About the authors 70

About the illustrator 72

Book chat 74

MEET THE BARBER BUS TEAM!

CHAPTER 1
Summer adventures

Hi, I'm Brodie.

When I was a baby, I was completely bald! I didn't have a single hair on my head. It took a long time for my hair to grow, but now I have the most amazing hair!

At the moment, my hair is very long, and long hair can be troublesome. I wear a hairband to keep it out of my eyes, just like a star footballer!

Every summer, I spend some of my school holidays with my grandma and grandpa. Mum is helping me pack my suitcase from the list I've made. I have a habit of forgetting the most important things. Once I even lost my list!

There's just enough room for everything I need, which must be packed very neatly. What I don't need is left safe and sound, everything in its place waiting for when I come back again.

My case will slot into place, right next to the toolbox, in the little gap of Mum's work van.

The butterflies in my stomach always begin to dance around when I'm heading off to see Grandma and Grandpa. Mum says it's the excitement. The butterflies in her stomach also do somersaults, as she's excited for me. We always miss each other when I go on my adventures with my grandparents, but my mum has some fun stuff to do with her friends, so we're glad for each other too.

Before we set off, Mum phoned Grandma and Grandpa to find out where they're living right now, because they don't live in one fixed place. We've written down the place and checked the way, so we know where we're going. We're heading there now!

Grandma and Grandpa have never lived in a house. They used to have a caravan but now they have a bus.

It's not just any bus, it's a Brilliant Barber Bus. It used to be an ordinary bus that took people from place to place.

It looks like an ordinary double-decker bus, and it still works to drive around, but inside it has been converted into Grandma and Grandpa's home and a barber shop – which gets lots of guests!

In the bus, I even have my own fold-down bed, which doubles as a den for me and Toady.

Oh! ... I nearly forgot! Toady always stays on the bus – you'll get to meet him later.

You'll also get to meet the customers, who love the Barber Bus coming to them. They say, "It's just brilliant!"

Just mind the step as you get on the bus.

That's the ticket machine – it still works. We use it to make hair appointment cards for the customers if they want a reminder. We punch a hole in the ticket when they visit again.

Not everyone wants a ticket, but if they're like me, it helps them to remember when the Brilliant Barber Bus will be returning. Some children like getting a ticket as they board the bus.

As we'll be on the road a lot, Grandma puts an extra ticket roll and some highlighters in the pouch there. Grandpa has fitted a little drop-down table, just like those you get on a plane!

If we want to listen to music, we can play it on my tablet. Grandpa and Grandma need to use the radio to listen to weather and traffic reports.

It's important to find out what the traffic and weather will be like, because the Brilliant Barber Bus must maintain its reputation – *Always on time!*

We can also track the weather using this app. Look – see that symbol of the cloud and two whirly lines? That means strong winds.

Let's leave our things on the luggage rack while we explore. It was a useful feature, so Grandma and Grandpa left the rack when they converted it from a passenger bus. Customers can leave their belongings there while they get their hair done.

Guess what? Grandma has stocked the refreshment station with some tasty snacks!

CHAPTER 2
Toady

When the Barber Bus is in action, we flick this switch to turn on our generator, which runs on recycled cooking oil and solar panels. This provides us with electricity wherever we go. These four switches are for the lights, the screen, the mini barber-plane ride for the little children and the sockets to power the hairstyling tools.

All the tools are stored back here on the trolley that we park beside the section we call the Glamorous Gallery.

Grandpa has a camera that can print out photographs, so he takes a snap of everyone who visits. All the photos get displayed in a big montage. Look, here's mine.

That reminds me, Grandpa keeps his camera with Toady, in the cubbyhole under the stairs to the upper deck.

Here's Toady, asleep in his box. You can hold him if you like – he won't bite.

Sometimes, children and adults can be a little wary of getting their hair cut and Grandpa says Toady has a calming effect when they hold him.

He's a piece of kidney ore that Grandma's Daddo found when he worked down the coalmine, not far from the village we're visiting later. Toady didn't pass the quality check of the mine, so Grandma's Daddo took him home and he's been with Grandma ever since.

You should see my collection of rocks, gems and fossils at home. Although I can identify and name lots of different kinds of rock, I always carry my little guidebook. That way, if I see an interesting rock while I'm on my travels, I can look it up and find out what it is.

Before going upstairs, I'll tell you a little bit about the people in the photo montage.

Samaran has got curly brown hair. He's a little older and taller than me, and he always brings his own collection of rocks to show me.

Samaran likes to lie on the floor with Toady and his rock collection, while he gets his hair cut. Grandpa cuts his hair using the "scissor-over-comb" technique, which is nice and quiet.

Grandma even made a catch-it-cape to stop any pieces of hair falling on the rocks.

This is Mrs Andrews and Ruby. Their picture is displayed lower down the wall so Ruby can see it, as Mrs Andrews says she's getting to be too heavy to lift up. With so many customers, we'll need a couple more pegs for all the photos.

Samaran

Mrs Andrews and Ruby

Grandpa always says, "Them pegs ain't like Uncle Cyril's." Uncle Cyril would whittle wood, using a knife, to make the pegs which he sold door to door as he travelled from place to place. His pegs were also popular with children who added scraps of cloth to them to make little dolls.

Here's the photo of Mr Armstrong. He likes to have a cup of tea before relaxing in the chair, to have his beard trimmed.

Mr Armstrong

This photo is of Mrs Gabour. She's got curly hair, called a perm. She says that her granddaughter, Mia, gets excited when the Barber Bus comes to town as she likes to ride the barber-plane. It used to be part of a merry-go-round that travelled with Grandpa's family funfair, when he was little.

Grandpa even installed a flip-down television that shows a picture of the sky, so it looks like the plane is flying through the clouds!

Mrs Gabour and Mia

So, while Mrs Gabour gets her curls set, Mia flies in the barber-plane getting her hair styled into a French braid.

We'll have to look at the rest of the photos later. Grandpa says we need to set off quickly. He's just had a message from Mr Allison, the leader of Cumbersdale Council, reminding him that there's an important party happening. They want the Brilliant Barber Bus to join them!

From here, it's a pretty straightforward trip to Cumbersdale. We'll be there in a couple of hours.

That sign tells us we need to put on our seatbelts.

CLICK. Off we go!

CHAPTER 3
To Cumbersdale!

Grandma has checked the weather forecast for today, and it isn't good, but we should get to the village of Cumbersdale well before the storm arrives.

She's also double-checked the map for low bridges. Choosing the roads carefully is very important as we have to avoid going under any bridges where the bus would get stuck.

We'll soon be turning off this main road, onto the country road, which will lead us directly to the village. Look at that windsock at the side of the road! I guess the wind's getting stronger. The double-decker bus is a tall vehicle and if it sways a lot in strong wind, there's a chance it could blow over. Hopefully, the wind won't get that strong!

No such luck! The wind is picking up quickly and now it's really blasting! I don't like the bus swaying – it feels like it's been hit by a barrage of air. I'm so pleased Grandma is a good driver; she's got the right technique to keep the bus going. But the howling noise of the wind is making me feel a little nervous.

Phew! We're now heading towards the section where the branches form an arc, which always reminds me of a tunnel.

In here, it's so much quieter and the bus feels a lot steadier. I can't hear the wind howling and whistling so much. I'm guessing that's because we're in the shelter of the trees. Or maybe the storm's died down or passed. I hope it's passed.

Until we get through the woods to
the open road again, we won't really know ...

SCREECH!

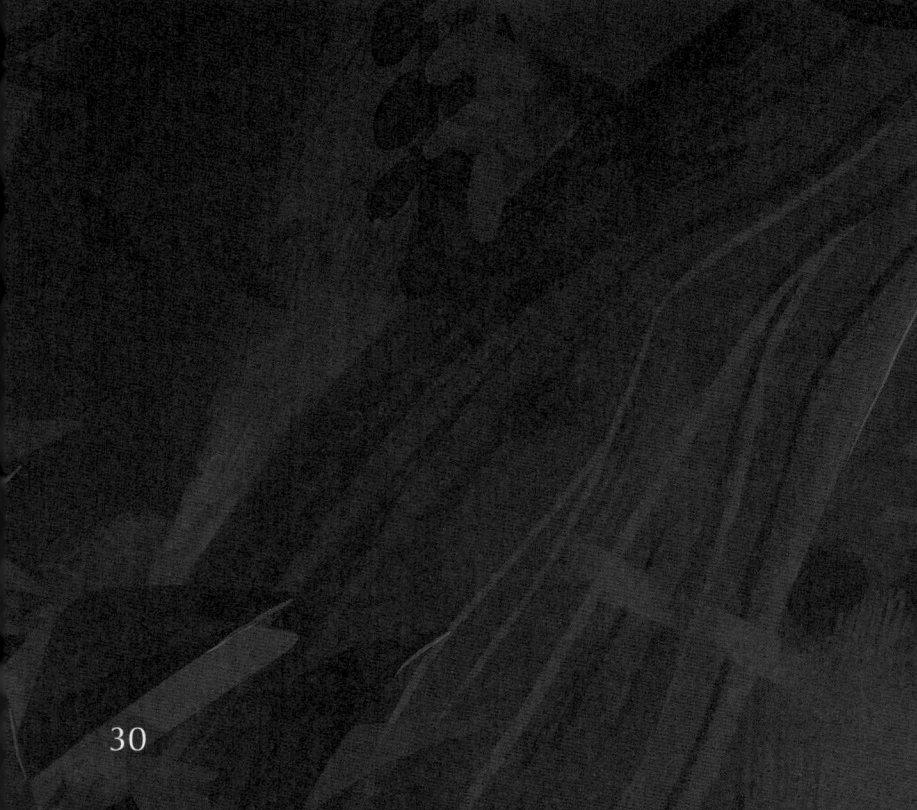

That was an abrupt stop! I wonder why Grandma had to slam on the brakes!

Look! An enormous tree is lying right across the road in front of the bus. Looking at it this closely, it's absolutely huge. It's strange to see a tree from this angle, with its roots all stuck up in the air.

We can undo our seatbelts when Grandma switches off the bus. Let's get up and see if there's any damage after that sharp stop. Just be careful, as some things may have fallen. We'll need to check if Toady is OK – that jolt could've thrown him out of his hidey-hole.

Look! Poor Toady has landed in a tub of strawberries!

We'll clean up Toady while Grandma salvages the rest of the strawberries.

Grandpa is going outside to take a closer look.

He's checked that it's safe and we can take a closer look at the tree. Grandpa knows all about trees and has identified this as an old English oak tree.

There's that whistling wind again, it sounds so eerie ...

CREAK ... CREAK ...

That tree further back up the road behind the bus is beginning to sway. It's leaning right over and looks like it will ...

CRACK!

THWUMP!

Yep! It's fallen. Wow! I'm glad it crashed down there away from our bus! When it bounced and hit the road, lots of small twigs and branches scattered everywhere.

A fallen tree in front of the bus and now a fallen tree behind!

We might be trapped for hours!

Grandpa is trying to phone Mr Allison, but it doesn't look like there's any phone reception. How will anyone know how to find us? What if another tree comes down right on top of us? What do we do now?!

Grandpa says not to worry, he's had a good look around at the remaining tall trees and he's worked out that, even if they came down, none would reach our vehicle. So we're safe, and the bus is safe.

We should probably head back there. The noise of the wind whistling through the trees is beginning to sound really creepy.

Grandma's asked us to keep Toady with us, so he'll feel safe. She calls us the Tenacious Trio who'll have a wonderful story to share about our windy adventures.

Just holding Toady makes me feel calmer.

CHAPTER 4
Trapped!

Looks like the sun is beginning to set. It'll be dark soon. Did you hear the sound of the owl hooting through the whistling wind?

Grandma says there's nothing for it right now but to sit and wait for the wind to die down. Grandpa's suggested it's time for a bit of cake and a warm drink. While we eat, I'll tell you more about our unique family and our Brilliant Barber Bus.

When Grandma was a child, she didn't go to school. Everything she learnt was from asking questions and watching the adults around her. She was part of a big family, and being the eldest, she had to help the younger children to get dressed and look smart in the mornings. She made sure her sisters' long hair looked neat. Her talents also came in handy for grooming the horses and braiding their manes. The horses would pull the wagons – one of her family's vardos (living wagons) is in the Carthorse Museum!

When Grandma was 17 years old, the family was parked up for the winter. A neighbour persuaded her to go to the local hairdressing school, which she did – and got top marks!

Grandma qualified as a hairdresser and opened her first hairdressing shop, near the mine where Toady was found. It was at the hairdressers that she met Grandpa. He came in, keen to have his hair cut.

It was the grand opening of the Marratown Charter Fair the next day. Grandpa wanted to look his best as he was giving a speech.

Grandpa was always very particular about his hair and Grandma gave him the perfect haircut.

He was so pleased with the experience that, as well as giving her a money tip, Grandpa persuaded Grandma to come to the fair and ask for him. He'd make sure she and her family got free rides on the Waltzer and Dodgems!

My grandparents became a couple and then got married. Together, they travelled with the fair where they learnt skills from each other. Grandma learnt how to drive trucks and Grandpa got experience cutting hair. Before too long, they decided to settle and open a barber shop in Brambleton. Grandpa went on a barbering course and soon they were both working in the shop and doing extremely well.

They had a baby (my mum), but by the time I was born, they were missing life on the open road. They were ready to travel again! So, they came up with the idea of creating the Barber Bus to help everyone who couldn't get to a barber or hairdresser.

With all the noises and machines, some people find it difficult to go a regular hairdressers, so Grandma and Grandpa's bus is a perfect alternative.

They found an old double-decker bus in a reclamation yard, which they converted into the Barber Bus. Grandpa has the skills that all Showmen learn – to create a place to live and work. There's plenty of room for me and Mum to stay whenever we want. The bus often travels to the same places that Grandpa's family fun fair still visits.

When the fair is around, I get to spend time with my cousins. So, just like when Grandpa was growing up, I'm learning how to weld and paint. Showmen need to know how to do these things, to maintain the equipment so it's safe for all the visitors.

Sometimes there are fairs, like Appleberry Horse Fair, where both Grandma and Grandpa's families attend. Then I spend time with other extended family members, learning different things like cooking flatbread on an open fire.

There are also football matches, family celebrations and Showman parties throughout the year.

This means that even though me and my mum are settled, we learn about the way of life that's shaped us. We get to spend time with our family and friends, too!

Talking of parties, I wonder if we've missed the Cumbersdale party.

Sadly, on this occasion, it looks like the Brilliant Barber Bus is not *Always on time!*

CHAPTER 5
Rescue

The wind has finally died down, but now it's getting dark. After all the warm drinks and stories, I'm beginning to feel sleepy. Grandma and Grandpa agree that we might as well stay here for the night now. I'll show you how to set up the fold-down bed.
If we're stuck here for the night, at least we'll be warm and cosy!

Hopefully it will be peaceful now the wind has settled ...

Vrrumm

What was that? It sounded like a machine. It's getting closer and louder.

VRRRRUM!

Look! There's a flashing light shining through the leaves of the fallen tree in front of us. I think it's a rescue vehicle!

Grandpa says that Mr Allison might have raised the alarm after we didn't show up. So the rescue team have come out to find us.

It looks like the rescue team are prepared. Those chainsaws are really noisy! I've a spare pair of headphones you can wear if you want. Wait here, I'll go and get them for you.

VRRRRUM!

JJWUMMP!

VRRRRUM!

JJWUMMP!

The team are quickly getting to work with chainsaws. They're chopping the fallen tree up into smaller chunks, so they can drag it to the sides of the road.

It really is noisy work. It looks like they've managed to clear the road! We can get going again! Let's go back down and put our seatbelts on.

Although there's enough room for the bus to pass, the rescue team say it's best if they lead the way, just in case any more trees have fallen. Grandma's driving technique will be tested once more as we snake past all the leaves and branches. Thankfully, the road looks clear, and we make our way slowly.

I ask Grandma if she thinks we'll be late for the party, but she says she thinks it will still be going on. She reckons it's better to arrive late than never.

Cumbersdale isn't that far away. The space between the trees is widening and moonlight is filtering through. Look! Triangles of bunting are fluttering from the branches. It looks like someone has been busy decorating the main road through the village.

Last time the village had a party, some people (like me) found the lights and noise all a bit too much. So, Grandma had suggested using the bus as a place for some quiet time. It was such a good idea that Grandpa had assured Mr Allison that they would do the same this time. We'll switch the fairy lights on by the barber-plane and and add some cosy blankets so it can be used as a quiet area. I think people will like that.

The rescue vehicle is indicating left – they are heading back to their base while we carry on to the village centre.

There don't seem to be many people about in the village – maybe we've missed the party after all!

We'll be parking up round the corner next to the village hall.

Look! There's a woman with a huge camera and a man with a microphone, and it looks like they're filming the bus – and us! I wonder what's happening.

I couldn't hear what they announced. Oops! That's because I forgot to take off my headphones. Now I've slipped them off, the words sound like they're booming out across the square. It's as if they're beckoning us inside the village hall.

And here we are – the village hall, the place where everyone is waiting for the party to start. We haven't missed the party after all!

Jeepers! Did you hear that?
Grandma and Grandpa have won an award for all the work they do in the community. We're not just attending the party, we're a key part of it! Everyone is cheering and congratulating us.

Look at the banner that the villagers have painted: *The Brilliant Barber Bus, Never Late and Always On Time!*

There are so many messages and photos underneath, all about Grandma and Grandpa.

Grandma says each picture holds a story, sparking a memory that she thought she'd forgotten.

CHAPTER 6
Guests of honour

It's so nice reading all the messages from the villagers! It's also fun to listen to Grandma and Grandpa talk about how the Barber Bus and the people who visit make them smile.

It reminds me of the Glamorous Gallery on the Barber Bus, but this time, it's all to honour my grandparents!

Here's Mr Allison coming towards us! He's wearing a big gold chain, as it's an important event. I think it makes him look like a rapper, but I'd better not say that to him as he might not like it.

He says he's saved us a seat right at the front of the hall. They've even put a special, bright-red mat on the table for Toady – he's become a big star in Cumbersdale.

I'd forgotten I'd put Toady in my pocket, so he's actually here too! Phew! I think Toady likes being a local celebrity.

Wow! Look at all the people gathered in the hall! There are so many! You'll recognise some of them from the photo montage.

Mr Allison has announced that he is going to play a film that was recorded earlier. The film is about everyone who visits the Barber Bus. They've all been interviewed about Grandma and Grandpa. What they say shows just how popular Grandma and Grandpa – and the Barber Bus – really are! Mrs Gabour says, "The bus is so much more than just a place to get your hair done – it's like a heartbeat that leaves a smile wherever it goes."

I wonder if Grandma and Grandpa are getting a feeling of butterflies or knots in their stomach. They've been asked to make a speech when they go up on the stage to receive their award. In front of all these people! I wouldn't like that. I'm getting a bit nervous for them. I'm so glad you and Toady are here.

I think the film crew were surprised when Grandma and Grandpa explained that they were born into two different kinds of Travelling communities. They said that each community shares a history of being helpful and bringing smiles to the places they visit.

Grandma told them about her Romani family, who lived and travelled in their traditional wooden vardos – wagons which were pulled by horses. They picked fruit and vegetables for farmers. Grandma's Uncle Cyril was a master at whittling wood, and he used to make pegs to sell. She told about how her mum and sister Violet showed her which hedgerow plants were safe to eat and when they were ripe to pick.

Grandpa shared stories of his Showman family bringing all the fun of the fair to towns and villages. While they were doing this work, away from their hometown, they stayed in a living wagon that had a door on the side. Everyone laughed and nodded when he told them about the convoy of wagons as they moved slowly along the country roads, creating as much interest as the fair itself!

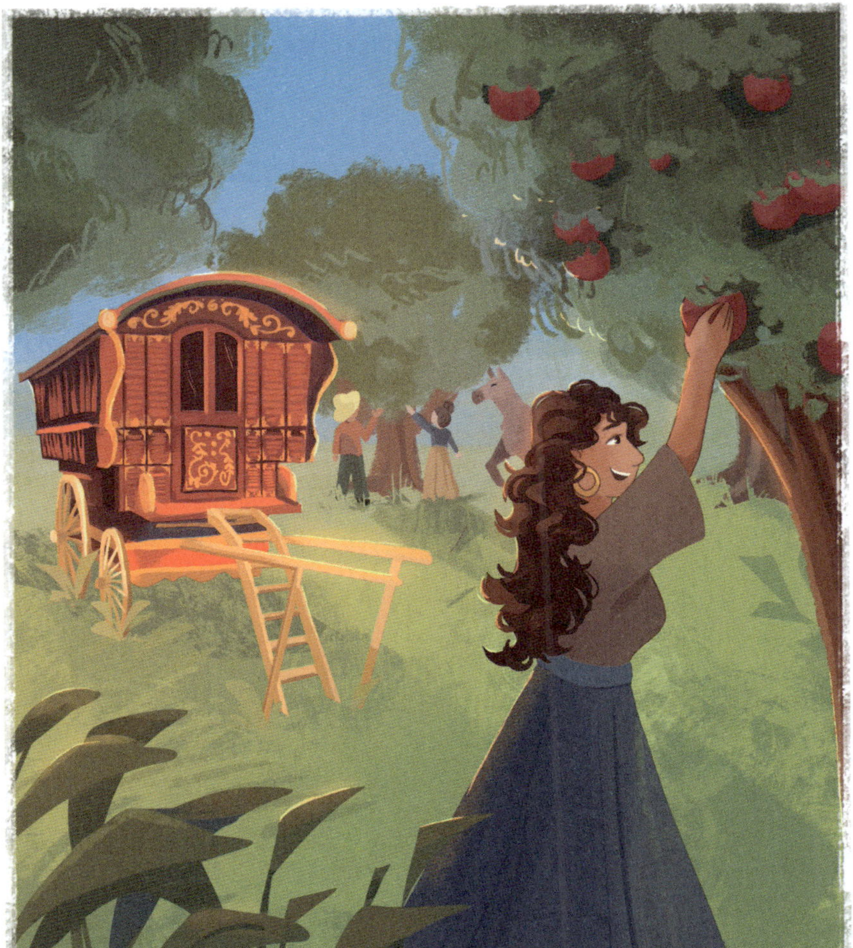

He talked about the smell of diesel-powered trucks and setting up the hooplas and sideshows, the food trucks and big daredevil rides. Who'd have thought that Grandpa once rode a motorcycle on the Wall of Death! I remember him joking that it should have been called the Wall of Noise because when he rode his motorbike around, the sound was deafening.

When I told him that I would just wear my ear defenders, he laughed.

Listening to their stories makes me think of all the things I've learnt from spending time with Grandma and Grandpa on the bus. They say that their history is my history, and it probably won't be found in any books, so I have to listen carefully.

A local reporter asked if they could visit the bus and Grandma said we'd be happy to show them around.

I think they'll see for themselves that our bus is not just any old bus, it's the Brilliant Barber Bus, with the most brilliant Grandma and Grandpa.

It is the Brilliant Barber Bus that travels from place to place and is *Always on time!*

THE BUS TRIP

- village of Cumbersdale, home of the Cumbersdale Pie
- travelling fair, location where Grandpa invited Grandma to visit
- iron ore mine where Grandma's Daddo found Toady, the piece of kidney ore
- Brodie's home, where he lives with his mum, Dakota
- Creamdale Ice Cream farm shop
- Appleberry carthorse museum
- hairdressers where Grandma met Grandpa
- where the Barber Bus gets trapped

	bridge		lake
	main road		woodland
	minor road		
	river		low bridge

Brambleton

Creamdale

Brambleside

Alstonberry

Renwitch

Edenvale

Cambrian

Appleberry

Cumbersdale

Rockford

Marratown

N / W / E / S

65

ALL KINDS OF HAIR
a poem by Brodie, Grandma and Grandpa

A short cut, a long braid. Curls with a hat.
Styled while you smile, with a cuppa and chat.
Clippers and scissors, both at the ready,
Skilled hands guiding, keeping them steady.
Curls set like a queen or spiked like a king,
A graduated bob that'll make your heart sing.
The Barber Bus seats people with all kinds of hair,
Grandma and Grandpa showing everyone
   they care.

Scissor-over-comb if the clipper's too loud,
A perm like a poodle or even a cloud!
Foils and extensions, ready for change,
The Barber Bus styles do every range.
A colour or tint, a blend of any shade,
A pixie or wedge, even a fade.
The Barber Bus seats people with all kinds of hair,
Grandma and Grandpa showing everyone
   they care.

Short back and sides, with a touch of gel,
Shaped to perfection or free-flowing well.
Feathered or layered, snip, snip, snip.
A new trend, a tricky cut, something that's *hip*.
Every technique, each skill acquired,
Grandma and Grandpa, both admired.
The Barber Bus seats people with all kinds of hair,
Grandma and Grandpa showing everyone
   they care.

TRAVELLER'S TALES

A traditional Showman's living wagon with Michelle's family

A traditional Roma's living wagon

Games and rides are a family business and they are passed down through generations.

Everyone in the family helps to set up their part of the fair ready for visitors.

The Russell family business: Bang Up To Date Amusements.

About the authors

Why did you want to be an author?

I fell in love with books from an early age and I thought being able to create them for other people to enjoy would be a very good thing to do.

Richard O'Neill

What is it like for you to write?

It's a great feeling of freedom.

Why did you decide to write this book?

So Michelle and I could give a different view of Travelling communities.

Do you own a pet rock like Toady?

Strangely enough I do have a piece of concrete I call my pet concrete . . . it's a long story how I came to have such a pet.

Is there a Barber Bus in real life? If not, do you think there should be?

There are lots of mobile hairdressers, but I don't think there is one exactly like ours and yes, there certainly should be!

How did you get into writing?

When my children were young I made books for them using photographs. I'd glue the photos into a notebook and add words and doodles to create stories. Becoming a professional writer is thanks to Richard, who asked me to co-author a story based on a Showman family.

Michelle Russell

What is a book you remember loving reading when you were young?

As a little girl, I remember my Mam taking me and my sister to choose books from the library. I loved the rhymes and pictures in *Each Peach Pear Plum*.

Is there anything in this book that relates to your own experiences?

Like Grandpa, my own heritage and family links to Travelling Showmen and the industry of funfairs. I'm told that my grandad built his own living wagon (caravan). Some of my family and friends are also hairdressers and barbers. Before I became an author I was a real bus driver, so I know exactly how Grandma might be feeling when she's driving through the storm.

About the illustrator

A bit about me …

I'm Jade, and I live in the Netherlands. I live with my husband and my 2 fluffy Norwegian forest cats. I really like watching movies, reading, cooking, and going to my pottery class.

Jade Van Der Zalm

How did you get into illustration?

When I was younger, I really did not like colouring. Not because I didn't like drawing, but because I wanted to tell my own stories. So, I used to flip the colouring page upside-down and draw my own stories on the back.

Is there anything in this book that relates to your own experiences?

I have very thick, straight, and dark hair. So, I have always had a hard time finding a good hairdresser. I love how Grandma and Grandpa always try to tailor their techniques to their customers and learn many new things because they travel around!

What was the most difficult thing about illustrating this book?

The most difficult thing for me was probably illustrating the Barber Bus. I could tell from the brief how much the authors had thought about the way it should look and feel. Everything had to be just right so it took me a while to work out how to do that in the best way possible!

How do you bring a character to life?

When illustrating characters, I always try to get to know them better. How would they move if they're walking or talking? Are they very calm or very expressive? Thinking about these details always helps with bringing a character to life!

Which character or scene did you most like drawing?

I liked illustrating the Barber Bus best! Even though it was also the most difficult, I liked figuring out how to bring the authors' ideas to life! The Barber Bus is also very cool. I really want to have a bus or caravan like that myself in the future to travel around in!

Did you have to do any research for this book?

Yes, absolutely! When illustrating any book, I always do a lot of research. For this book I looked up many pictures on what buses look like but also the tools hairdressers use and how you should hold scissors.

Book chat

Which part of the book did you like best, and why?

Does the book remind you of any other books you've read? How?

Would you like to get your hair cut on the Barber Bus? Why or why not?

Do any characters in the book remind you of someone you know in real life? If so, how?

Which character in the book did you think was most interesting? Why?

What did you think of the book at the start? Did you change your mind at all as you read it?

If you could talk to one of the characters, who would you pick? What would you say to them?

Would you like to read another book that follows on from this one? If so, what might be in it?

If you had to pick one scene to act out, which would you choose? Why?

Book challenge:

Design your own amazing bus. What would you use it for?

Collins
BIG CAT

Published by Collins
An imprint of HarperCollins*Publishers*
The News Building
1 London Bridge Street
London SE1 9GF
UK

Macken House
39/40 Mayor Street Upper
Dublin 1
D01 C9W8
Ireland

© HarperCollins*Publishers* Limited 2023

10 9 8 7 6

ISBN 978-0-00-862468-2

All rights reserved. No part of this publication may be reproduced, stored in a retrieval system, or transmitted in any form by any means, electronic, mechanical, photocopying, recording or otherwise, without the prior written permission of the Publisher or a licence permitting restricted copying in the United Kingdom issued by the Copyright Licensing Agency Ltd, 5th Floor, Shackleton House, 4 Battle Bridge Lane, London SE1 2HX.

British Library Cataloguing-in-Publication Data
A catalogue record for this publication is available from the British Library.

Download the teaching notes and word cards to accompany this book at:
http://littlewandle.org.uk/signupfluency/

Get the latest Collins Big Cat news at
collins.co.uk/collinsbigcat

Authors: Richard O'Neill and Michelle Russell
Illustrator: Jade Van Der Zalm (Astound Illustration Agency)
Publisher: Lizzie Catford
Product manager and commissioning editor: Caroline Green
Series editor: Charlotte Raby
Development editor: Catherine Baker
Project manager: Emily Hooton
Content editor: Daniela Mora Chavarría
Phonics reviewer: Rachel Russ
Copyeditor: Catherine Dakin
Proofreader: Gaynor Spry
Typesetter: 2Hoots Publishing Services Ltd
Cover designer: Sarah Finan
Production controller: Katharine Willard

Collins would like to thank the teachers and children at the following schools who took part in the trialling of Big Cat for Little Wandle Fluency: Burley And Woodhead Church of England Primary School; Chesterton Primary School; Lady Margaret Primary School; Little Sutton Primary School; Parsloes Primary School.

Printed and bound in the UK

MIX
Paper | Supporting responsible forestry
FSC™ C007454
www.fsc.org

This book contains FSC™ certified paper and other controlled sources to ensure responsible forest management.

For more information visit:
www.harpercollins.co.uk/green

Acknowledgements
The publishers gratefully acknowledge the permission granted to reproduce the copyright material in this book. Every effort has been made to trace copyright holders and to obtain their permission for the use of copyright material. The publishers will gladly receive any information enabling them to rectify any error or omission at the first opportunity.

pp68t & 69 courtesy of Michelle Russell, p68b courtesy of Richard O'Neill.